Tuba

FILM FAVORITES

Solos and Band Arrangements
Correlated with Essential Elements® Band Method

Arranged by
MICHAEL SWEENEY, JOHN MOSS and PAUL LAVENDER

Welcome to ESSENTIAL ELEMENTS FILM FAVORITES! The arrangements in this versatile book can be used either in a full concert band setting or as solos for individual instruments. The SOLO pages appear at the beginning of the book, followed by the BAND ARRANGEMENT pages. The supplemental CD recording or PIANO ACCOMPANIMENT book may be used as an accompaniment for solo performance.

ISBN 978-0-634-08704-2

HAL•LEONARD® CORPORATION
7777 W. BLUEMOUND RD. P.O. BOX 13819 MILWAUKEE, WI 53213

00860154

From Walt Disney Pictures' PIRATES OF THE CARIBBEAN: THE CURSE OF THE BLACK PEARL

PIRATES OF THE CARIBBEAN

(A medley including: The Medallion Calls • The Black Pearl)

TUBA
Solo

Music by KLAUS BADELT
Arranged by MICHAEL SWEENEY

00860154

From the Paramount and Twentieth Century Fox Motion Picture TITANIC

MY HEART WILL GO ON

(Love Theme From 'Titanic')

Music by JAMES HORNER
Lyric by WILL JENNINGS
Arranged by JOHN MOSS

TUBA
Solo

From THE MUPPET MOVIE

THE RAINBOW CONNECTION

TUBA
Solo

Words and Music by
PAUL WILLIAMS and **KENNETH L. ASCHER**
Arranged by PAUL LAVENDER

From THE LORD OF THE RINGS: THE FELLOWSHIP OF THE RING

MAY IT BE

TUBA
Solo

Words and Music by EITHNE NI BHRAONAIN,
NICKY RYAN and ROMA RYAN

Arranged by JOHN MOSS

00860154

From Walt Disney Pictures' TARZAN™

YOU'LL BE IN MY HEART

TUBA
Solo

Words and Music by
PHIL COLLINS
Arranged by MICHAEL SWEENEY

00860154

From the Motion Picture SHREK 2

ACCIDENTALLY IN LOVE

TUBA
Solo

Words and Music by
ADAM F. DURITZ
Arranged by MICHAEL SWEENEY

Moderate Rock

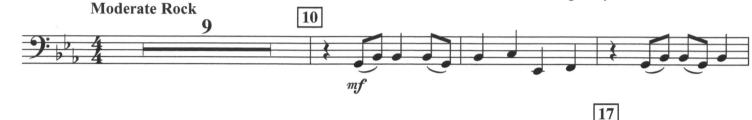

Featured in the Motion Picture 2001: A SPACE ODYSSEY

ALSO SPRACH ZARATHUSTRA

By RICHARD STRAUSS
Arranged by MICHAEL SWEENEY

TUBA
Solo

From the Paramount Motion Picture MISSION: IMPOSSIBLE

MISSION: IMPOSSIBLE THEME

TUBA
Solo

By LALO SCHIFRIN
Arranged by MICHAEL SWEENEY

From SHREK
MUSIC FROM SHREK
(A medley including: Fairytale Opening • Ride The Dragon)

TUBA
Solo

Music by JOHN POWELL
and HARRY GREGSON-WILLIAMS
Arranged by JOHN MOSS

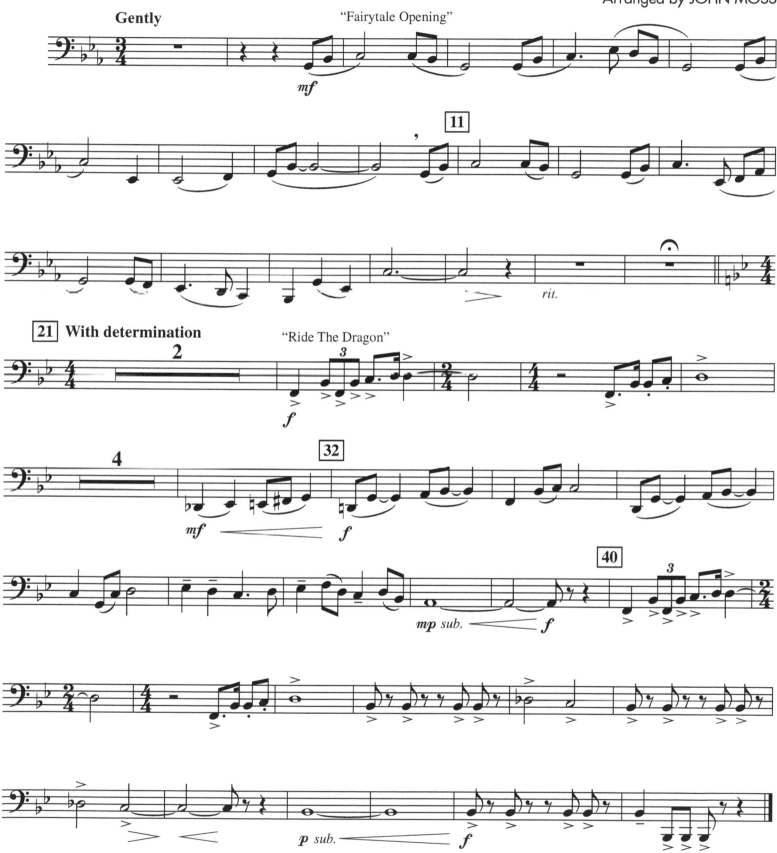

00860154

From the TriStar Motion Picture THE MASK OF ZORRO

ZORRO'S THEME

Composed by
JAMES HORNER
Arranged by JOHN MOSS

TUBA
Solo

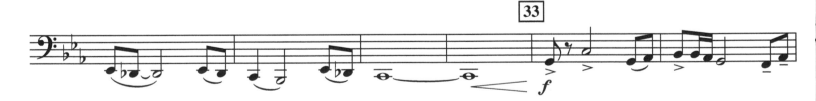

PIRATES OF THE CARIBBEAN

(A medley including: The Medallion Calls • The Black Pearl)

TUBA
Band Arrangement

Music by **KLAUS BADELT**
Arranged by **MICHAEL SWEENEY**

00860154

From the Paramount and Twentieth Century Fox Motion Picture TITANIC

MY HEART WILL GO ON

(Love Theme From 'Titanic')

Music by JAMES HORNER
Lyric by WILL JENNINGS
Arranged by JOHN MOSS

TUBA
Band Arrangement

00860154

From THE MUPPET MOVIE

THE RAINBOW CONNECTION

TUBA
Band Arrangement

Words and Music by
PAUL WILLIAMS and KENNETH L. ASCHER
Arranged by PAUL LAVENDER

From THE LORD OF THE RINGS: THE FELLOWSHIP OF THE RING

MAY IT BE

TUBA
Band Arrangement

Words and Music by EITHNE NI BHRAONAIN,
NICKY RYAN and ROMA RYAN
Arranged by JOHN MOSS

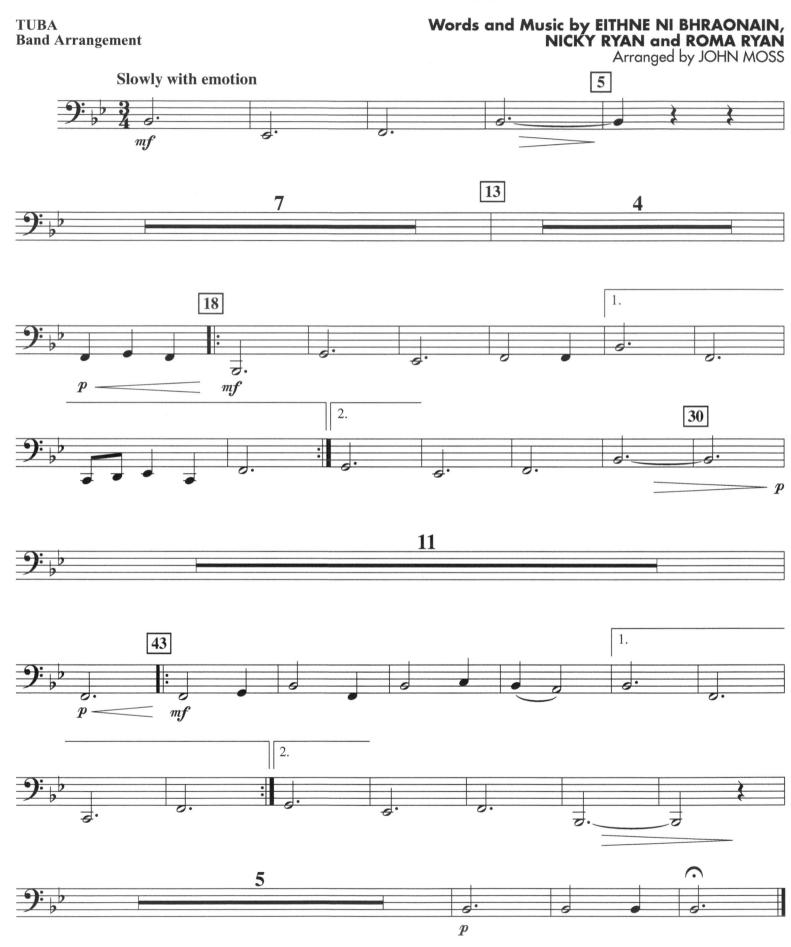

From Walt Disney Pictures' TARZAN™
YOU'LL BE IN MY HEART

TUBA
Band Arrangement

Words and Music by
PHIL COLLINS
Arranged by MICHAEL SWEENEY

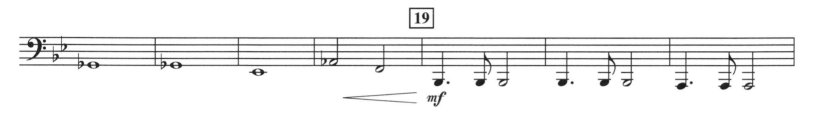

00860154

From the Motion Picture SHREK 2

ACCIDENTALLY IN LOVE

TUBA
Band Arrangement

Words and Music by
ADAM F. DURITZ
Arranged by MICHAEL SWEENEY

ALSO SPRACH ZARATHUSTRA

TUBA
Band Arrangement

By **RICHARD STRAUSS**
Arranged by MICHAEL SWEENEY

00860154

From the Paramount Motion Picture MISSION: IMPOSSIBLE

MISSION: IMPOSSIBLE THEME

TUBA
Band Arrangement

By LALO SCHIFRIN
Arranged by MICHAEL SWEENEY

From SHREK
MUSIC FROM SHREK
(A medley including: Fairytale Opening • Ride The Dragon)

Music by JOHN POWELL and HARRY GREGSON-WILLIAMS
Arranged by JOHN MOSS

TUBA
Band Arrangement

From the TriStar Motion Picture THE MASK OF ZORRO

ZORRO'S THEME

Composed by JAMES HORNER
Arranged by JOHN MOSS

TUBA
BAND ARRANGEMENT

Heroically

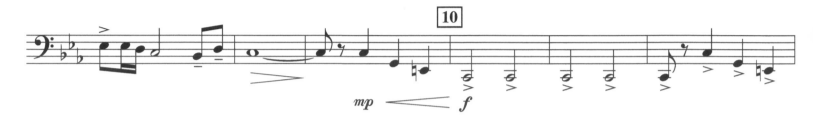

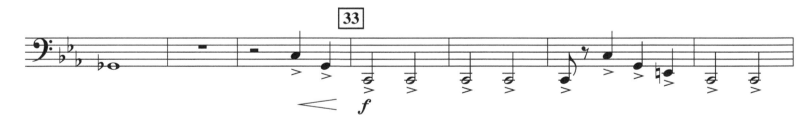

MORE FAVORITES FROM ESSENTIAL ELEMENTS

Each song appears twice in the book, featuring:
- Solo instrument version
- Band arrangement for full band or ensembles
- Pop-style accompaniment CD included with conductor's score
- Accompaniment CD available separately
- Piano accompaniment book that is compatible with recorded backgrounds

Prices:
- Conductor Books $24.99
- Instrument Books $6.99
- Piano Accompaniment Books $11.99
- Accompaniment CDs. $12.99

These superb collections feature favorite songs that students can play as they progress through their band method books. Each song is arranged to be played by either a full band or by individual soloists, with optional accompaniment on CD.

Instrument books for each collection feature separate books for the following: Flute, Oboe, Bassoon, B♭ Clarinet, E♭ Alto Clarinet, B♭ Bass Clarinet, E♭ Alto Saxophone, B♭ Tenor Saxophone, E♭ Baritone Saxophone, B♭ Trumpet, F Horn, Trombone, Baritone B.C., Baritone T.C., Tuba, Percussion, and Keyboard Percussion.

BROADWAY FAVORITES
Arranged by Michael Sweeney
Songs include:
Beauty and the Beast
Tomorrow
Cabaret
Edelweiss
Don't Cry for Me Argentina
Get Me to the Church on Time
I Dreamed a Dream
Go Go Go Joseph
Memory
The Phantom of the Opera
Seventy Six Trombones

CHRISTMAS FAVORITES
Arranged by Michael Sweeney
Songs include:
The Christmas Song
 (Chestnuts Roasting on an Open Fire)
Frosty the Snow Man
A Holly Jolly Christmas
Jingle-Bell Rock
Let It Snow! Let It Snow! Let It Snow!
Rockin' Around the Christmas Tree
Rudolph, the Red-Nosed Reindeer.

FILM FAVORITES
Arranged by Michael Sweeney, John Moss and Paul Lavender
Songs include:
The Black Pearl
Fairytale Opening
Mission: Impossible Theme
My Heart Will Go On
Zorro's Theme
Music from Shrek
May It Be
The Medallion Calls
You'll Be in My Heart
The Rainbow Connection
Accidentally in Love
Also Sprach Zarathustra

MOVIE FAVORITES
Arranged by Michael Sweeney
Includes themes from:
An American Tail
Back to the Future
Chariots of Fire
Apollo 13
E.T.
Forrest Gump
Dances with Wolves
Jurassic Park
The Man from Snowy River
Raiders of the Lost Ark
Star Trek

PATRIOTIC FAVORITES
Arranged by Michael Sweeney
Songs include:
America, the Beautiful
Armed Forces Salute
Battle Hymn of the Republic
God Bless America
Hymn to the Fallen
My Country, 'Tis of Thee (America)
The Patriot
The Star Spangled Banner
Stars and Stripes Forever
This Is My Country
Yankee Doodle/Yankee Dookle Boy

THE BEATLES
Arranged by Robert Longfield, Johnnie Vinson and John Moss
Songs include:
And I Love Her
A Hard Day's Night
Yesterday
Get Back
Lady Madonna
Twist and Shout
Hey Jude
Eleanor Rigby
Ticket to Ride
Here, There and Everywhere
I Want to Hold Your Hand

Visit Hal Leonard Online at **www.halleonard.com**

Prices, contents, and availability subject to change without notice.
Some products may not be available outside the U.S.A.